5445 2726

EASY MIND and BODY TRICKS

beginner magic

Stephanie Turnbull

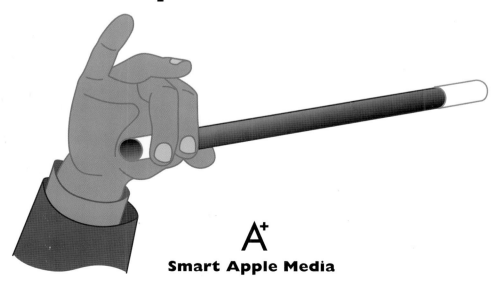

A+

Smart Apple Media

Published by Smart Apple Media, an imprint of Black Rabbit Books
P.O. Box 3263, Mankato, Minnesota, 56002
www.blackrabbitbooks.com

Printed in the United States of America, at Corporate Graphics
in North Mankato, Minnesota.

Designed and illustrated by Guy Callaby
Edited by Mary-Jane Wilkins

Library of Congress Cataloging-in-Publication Data

Turnbull, Stephanie.
  Easy mind and body tricks / Stephanie Turnbull.
     pages cm. -- (Beginner magic)
  Includes index.
  ISBN 978-1-62588-011-6
  1. Magic tricks--Juvenile literature. I. Title.
  GV1548.T86 2014
  793.8--dc23
                            2012051828

Photo acknowledgements
t = top, b = bottom
page 2 iStockphoto/Thinkstock,
4 alexkatkov/Shutterstock; 5t Stocksnapper/
Shutterstock, b Borislav Toskov/Shutterstock;
page 11 Steve Collender/Shutterstock;
page 20 iStockphoto/Thinkstock
Cover images
spoon Big Pants Production/Shutterstock, blocks and
wand Comstock, face Hemera, red curtain iStockphoto/
all Thinkstock

DAD0508
052013
9 8 7 6 5 4 3 2 1

Contents

Making Magic

You don't need expensive props to perform fantastic magic tricks—you just need yourself! The illusions in this book are easy to learn, quick to do, and make you look amazing.

Tips and ideas

Look out for these boxes as you read this book. They're full of handy tips for making tricks work perfectly.

If you're athletic, try combining body tricks with dance, mime or gymnastic displays.

4

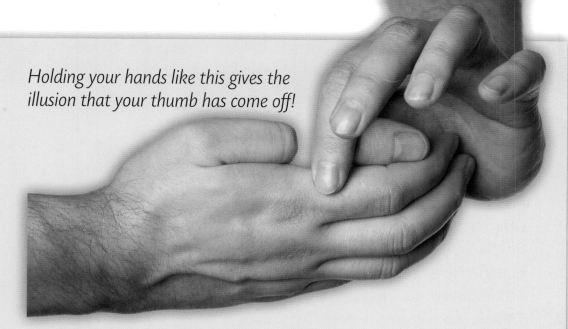

Holding your hands like this gives the illusion that your thumb has come off!

That's impossible!

You move or hold your body in sneaky ways to do some tricks, and use scientific laws of forces and lifting for others. They all fool people into thinking something impossible is happening right before their eyes.

Magic Secrets

You can also discover the secrets of master magicians... but don't tell anyone!

Show time

Even simple tricks need lots of practice—and they only work well if you perform confidently. Do lots of acting so people believe you're really stretching your body or controlling their mind!

Try wearing a spooky costume to perform mind tricks.

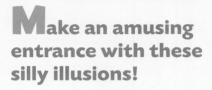

Make an amusing entrance with these silly illusions!

1. Hide behind a doorway and lean on the wall. Stand on one leg and bend over as far as you can, so the top half of your body is sideways.

2. Pretend to cling to the door frame as someone tries to pull your legs away!

Help! They've got me!

Aaargh!

3. Act as if you're being dragged away, then slide out of view altogether.

4. Now disguise one arm by rolling up a sleeve and putting on a glove. Pop your head around the door, keeping the changed arm hidden.

What...? Oh no!

Sorry about that. I think I shook him off...

5. As you talk, grab your neck with your other hand. Look surprised as the hand pulls you back behind the door!

Add fake fight sounds to make everyone laugh.

Keep your elbow hidden.

Magic Hands

Here are a couple of easy illusions using a wand. A pen or pencil with rounded sides works just as well.

1. Show the wand to a friend.

2. Now say that it will turn to rubber in your amazing magic hand. Hold it loosely at one end and wiggle it up and down rapidly. Don't shake it too hard.

You'll be surprised how effective this looks!

Magic Secrets

Magicians often wave a wand to distract your attention from their other hand.

8

3. Next, say that you'll use your magic hand to move the wand—without touching it. Place it carefully on the table and rub or flex your hand dramatically.

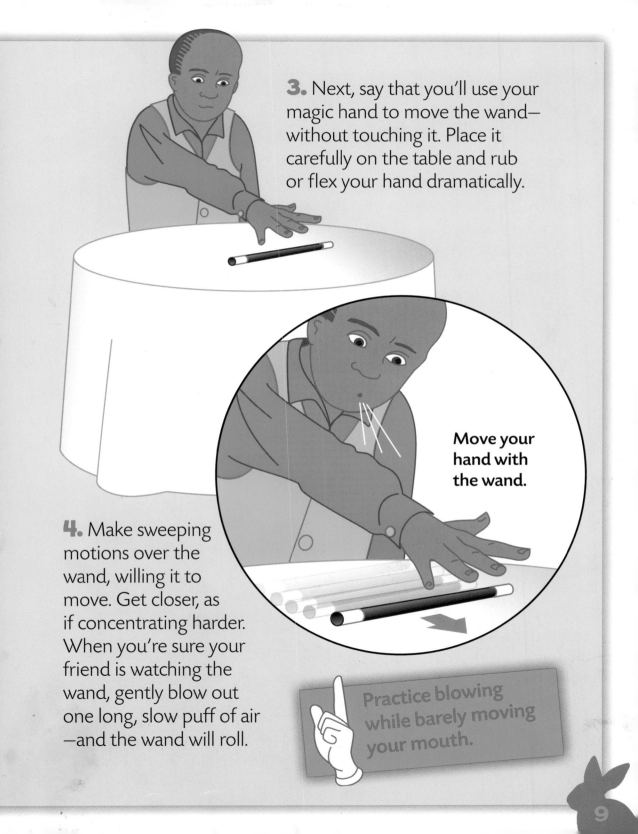

Move your hand with the wand.

4. Make sweeping motions over the wand, willing it to move. Get closer, as if concentrating harder. When you're sure your friend is watching the wand, gently blow out one long, slow puff of air —and the wand will roll.

Practice blowing while barely moving your mouth.

Stretchy Thumb

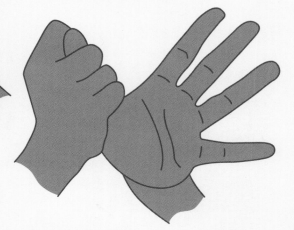

This effect is very realistic—try it in front of a mirror and see.

1. Tell a friend you have amazingly stretchy thumbs!

2. Grab your left thumb in your right fist—at the same time putting your right thumb between your first and middle fingers.

Here's your view:

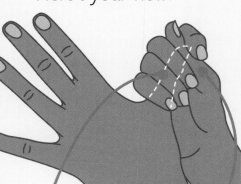

Left thumb hidden inside fist.

Right thumb between right fingers.

And here's what your friend sees from the other side:

The thumb looks connected to the rest of this hand—but it isn't.

3. Pretend to pull hard on the thumb with your fist. Slowly move your right hand up, so your thumb seems to stretch...

and stretch...

... until just the tip of your left thumb is hidden in your fist.

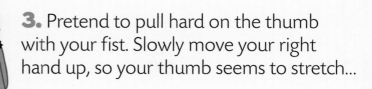

Aaaaaargh!

Wiggle your right thumb and left fingers so they seem connected.

Magic Secrets

Some magicians secretly squeeze out fake blood to pretend they're really injuring themselves!

Slowly move your fist back down again to return your thumb to its normal size.

Amazing Arms

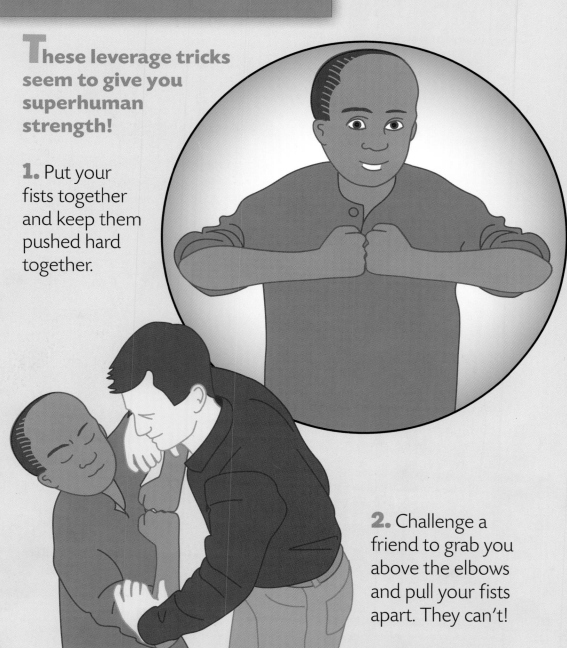

These leverage tricks seem to give you superhuman strength!

1. Put your fists together and keep them pushed hard together.

2. Challenge a friend to grab you above the elbows and pull your fists apart. They can't!

3. Tell another friend to sit in a chair without arms. Make sure they lean back with their hands on their knees and both feet in front of the chair.

4. Say that you can keep them in the chair using one super-strong arm. Stretch out and press your thumb on their forehead. Challenge them to stand. They can't!

The bigger your friends, the better this looks.

Now pretend your mind is just as powerful as your body.

1. Ask a friend to stand with their left side and left foot pressed against a wall. Say that you can control their body.

2. Point at their right foot and tell them to try lifting it off the ground for five seconds. They can't!

3. Next, tell your friend to press their left arm firmly against the wall. As they push, slowly count to 20.

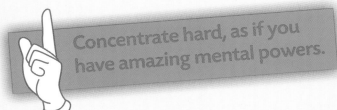

Concentrate hard, as if you have amazing mental powers.

4. Now ask them to move away from the wall and let their arms hang relaxed at their sides.

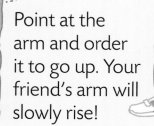

Point at the arm and order it to go up. Your friend's arm will slowly rise!

Magic Secrets

Your friend's arm rises because their muscles continue to push outward, even when the wall isn't there. Try it yourself!

Mind-Reading Test

This mind-reading trick is risky, because you have to hope your friend will pick an obvious answer—but they probably will!

1. Ask a friend to think of a number between one and ten.

2. Tell them to multiply it by nine. If the answer is two digits, they should then add the two numbers.

3

3 x 9 = 27

2 + 7 = 9

They don't know it, but they'll always get the number nine.

3. Now tell them to take away five and think of the letter of the alphabet that corresponds to their answer (1 = A, 2 = B, and so on).

9 – 5 = 4

4 = D

You know this will be D.

4. Next, ask them to think of a country beginning with that letter. Most people choose Denmark as it's the most obvious choice.

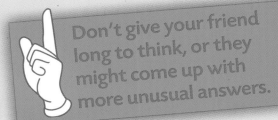

Don't give your friend long to think, or they might come up with more unusual answers.

5. Ask them to take the second letter in the name and think of an animal beginning with that letter...

Denmark

Elephant

Several animals begin with E, but one is more obvious than others!

6. ... then concentrate on the animal's color. Pretend to read their mind and announce the color you 'see'!

Gray!

Bending by Brain Power

Pretending to bend spoons is a classic mind and body trick. Here's one version.

1. Under the table, secretly hold a dime in your left hand like this. Don't let your friend see it.

2. Take a teaspoon in the other hand and show your friend it's an ordinary one.

3. Grab the spoon with both hands, with your left hand at the top. As you do this, push up the coin slightly, so it looks like the top of the handle.

Overlap your hands, so the spoon doesn't look too long.

Magic Secrets

Magicians use sneaky moves to 'bend' metal, such as hiding bent spoons in their hands or weakening the handle beforehand.

4. Rest the spoon on the table. Slowly press forward, letting the handle slide down through your hands. From the front, the handle seems to bend.

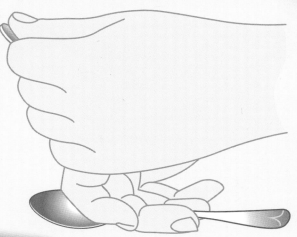

Here's the side view.

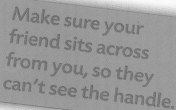

Make sure your friend sits across from you, so they can't see the handle.

5. When you've "bent" the spoon as far as you can, say, ***"And now I... unbend it!"*** and suddenly toss it onto the table.

Drop the coin on your lap while your friend studies the spoon.

19

Try this fantastic levitation trick in a dimly-lit room or outdoors in fading light.

1. Stand in an open space at a distance from a friend— for example, on the other side of the room. Make sure that most of your left foot, apart from the heel, is hidden from your friend.

Magic Secrets

Magicians who hover or fly high in the air use very thin wires or hidden supports.

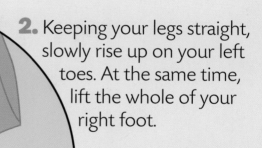

2. Keeping your legs straight, slowly rise up on your left toes. At the same time, lift the whole of your right foot.

Keep your heels together and your left toes hidden.

This is what your friend sees—both feet rising above the ground. It's only a tiny lift, but it can look really impressive.

3. Hold it for a couple of seconds, then slowly lower your feet again. Pretend to be exhausted after all that mental strain!

Don't "float" for long, and never do it twice—once the surprise has worn off, your friend may spot the trick.

digit
A figure from 0 to 9 that may be part of a bigger number.

hypnotize
To put someone in a kind of trance, in which they can be persuaded to alter their behavior or thoughts.

illusion
Something that seems impossible.

leverage
Forcing something to move or lift by working like a lever. Leverage tricks work because the muscles your friend has to use don't work very well as a lever for moving or lifting.

levitation
Making something seem to rise and hover in the air in a way that looks impossible.

mentalist
A kind of magician who performs tricks that seem to involve amazing mental power, such as reading minds.

probability
A measurement of how likely it is that something will happen in a certain situation.

prop
Any object you use to help perform a trick.

wand
A magic prop. Some wands are just for show. Others have secret moving parts or hollow spaces for hiding objects.

Magic Web Sites

To learn more about mind and body magic and try extra tricks, visit these helpful web sites:

www.ehow.com/info_8057910_easy-body-magic-tricks.html

www.escapadedirect.com/plwigr.html

www.instructables.com/id/Mathemagic

Index